THROUGH TIME AND SPACE

A COLLECTION OF POEMS BY CHY COX

Copyright © 2024 Poets Underground Press LLC

All rights reserved.

Poets Underground Press LLC
poetsundergroundpress.com

Publication by
Poets Underground Press LLC
on December 1st, 2024

All Poems by (The Writer): Chy Cox
Cover Design & All Illustrations by: Tris Seda

No part of this book may be reproduced, stored in a retrieval system or transmitted by any means without the consent of the Publisher and/or the Writer.

The views expressed in this book of poems are solely those of the Writer and do not necessarily reflect the views of the Publisher, and the Publisher hereby disclaims any responsibility for them.

ISBN: 979-8-218-53986-3

Table of Contents

Foreword   13-14

Mental Health

- The Voice In My Head (2023)   16
- How Are You Doing? (2023)   17

Grief

- Grief (2022)   19-20
- Survivor's Guilt (2022)   21-22
- Angel Numbers (2022)   23-26

Austin

- Austin (2022)   29-30
- Fentanyl (2022)   31-34
- I Don't Want Them (2022)   35-36

- One Year (2022)   37-38
- June 23rd (2022)   39-40
- It Wasn't Supposed To Be This Way (2023)   41-42
- A Secret (2024)   43-44
- Naloxone Can Reverse Opioid Overdose (2024)   45

In Loving Memory

- The Forget Me Nots (2022)   47-48
- Thomas (2022)   49
- Grandma Toni (2022)   50
- It Doesn't End (2022)   51-53
- Why It Matters (2022)   54
- We Deserve To Live (2022)   55-59

Growth, Healing, and Self-Love

- Blur (2011)   61
- Blur, Part II (2022)   62
- A Love Letter To Myself (2022)   63-64

- 27 (2022)   65-66
- I'm Happy You're Here (2023)   67-68
- I'm In Love (2023)   69-71
- Beyond Survival (2023)   72-73
- 28 (2023)   74-76
- The Best Is Yet To Come (2024)   77
- I'm In Love, Revisited (2024)   78-80

The Journey Home

- I Don't Agree (2022)   82
- There Is No Closet (2022)   83-87
- I'm A Lesbian (2022)   88-89
- The Fog (2023)   90-91
- Bloom (2023)   92
- I'm Headed That Way Too (2023)   93-94
- Thank You, Faint Voice (2024)   95-96

Trans: An Evolution in Self-Acceptance

- Gender (2022) — 98-99
- Trans (2023) — 100
- Deadname (2023) — 101-102
- Trans, Part II (2023) — 103-104
- Trans, Part III (2023) — 105
- Blissfully Chy (2023) — 106-108
- Not Anymore (2023) — 109
- I'm Not Dead Yet (2024) — 110-111
- House Of Cards (2024) — 112
- I Can't Keep This To Myself (2024) — 113-114

The Sapphic Series

- I Still Believe (2021) — 116
- I'm Sorry (2022) — 117
- For My Love (2022) — 118
- Haunted By Your Ghost (2022) — 119-120
- ▮ (2022) — 121

- ███, Part II (2022)   122-123
- ███ (2023)   124
- Love (2023)   125
- You're Safe With Me (2023)   126-127
- One Night Walk (2023)   128
- Crave (2023)   129
- But She's Out There (2023)   130-131

Heartbreak and Relational Healing

- You Don't Deserve Another Poem (2022)   133
- ███ (2023)   134
- The Parking Lot (2023)   135
- The Aftermath (2023)   136-137
- Extinguished (2023)   138
- Healing (2023)   139
- "You're A Handful" (2023)   140-141
- When (2023)   142
- Trauma (2023)   143
- "I Could Never Hate You" (2023)   144

- Ashes (2023)   145
- Ashes, Part II (2023)   146
- Chasing (2023)   147
- Simply Not True (2023)   148-149
- I Could Never Hate You (2023)   150-151
- The Inside Joke (2023)   152
- Crawling Out Of Love (2023)   153-154
- The Sword & The Shield (2023)   155
- The Four Walls (2023)   156-158
- You Could Never Lose Me (2023)   159
- It Has To Be Forever (2023)   160
- ███, Epilogue (2023)   161-162
- Imagine (2023)   163-164
- Walk Away (2023)   165
- If Looks Could Kill (2024)   166
- Pull The Plug (Again and Again) (2024)   167-169

Community and Friendship

- Where Are You? (2023)   171
- Kathryn (2023)   172-173
- "I Hope You Have Someone Good" (2023)   174-176
- What I Want My Friends To Know (2023)   177-179
- Community (2024)   180
- Alien (2024)   181-182

Love as a Lens

- Untitled (2022)   184-185
- I Get Angry (2022)   186-189
- Miracles (2023)   190
- How Can I Explain? (2023)   191
- When It Rains (2024)   192-194
- "Be Grateful It's Not You" (2024)   195-196
- At The Altar Of A New World (2024)   197-198

Wrapping Up (Uncategorized)

- Dad (2021) — 200
- Ryan (2022) — 201
- Serena's Lesson (2022) — 202-204
- Eggshells (2023) — 205
- I Hope You Tell Them (2023) — 206-208
- Small Things (2023) — 209
- Radical Dreamers (2023) — 210
- I'm Not Afraid (2024) — 211-212

Acknowledgements — 213-214

Meet the Author — 215-216

Meet the Publisher — 218

Index — 219

"These words are all I have, so I write them"

Fall Out Boy

This one's for me.

Foreword

Dear Reader,

It is a tremendous honor and a dream come true that you are reading this book. This book is a culmination of writing that spans more than a decade. Though most of my earlier writing from my teenage years did not make it into this book, those poems set me on the path I find myself today.

Poetry has been an integral part of my life's journey. It's more than a creative outlet; it's a way to process my emotions, a love language, a time capsule. These poems are an abridged chronicle of my journey through time and space so far. These pages contain my heart and soul.

At its core, this book is about connection. Over the years I've come to find that my poetry helps me connect with the different iterations of myself. Now, it will help me connect with you through time and space. I hope you can find something within these pages that speaks to you, that can shift your perspective, that makes you smile, that makes you feel less alone. Take what you need and leave out all the rest.

The names of people in my life that appear in this book do so with the permission of that person, with the exception of those that died before the book was written. I've chosen to include the names of my deceased loved ones as a way to honor them. All names of living people that I did not receive consent to include have been edited out or redacted for privacy.

In the case of my own name, my given name will appear throughout this book. I've made peace with the fact that this name will be known, but including it here is not equivalent to consenting to it being used. I ask that Chy be the name you use for me, as it is my chosen name and the name that affirms me.

This book contains themes that may be distressing to some readers. These themes include addiction, death, overdose, gun violence, homophobia, transphobia, and suicidal ideation.

Chapter 1

MENTAL HEALTH

*... every moment
is both a struggle
and a miracle*

The Voice In My Head

I'm not doing well today
The voice in my head
is telling me
that I'm better off dead
that it'll all be easier that way

I try to tell them
"No, it would be hard for the people that love me"
Who loves you?
they mock
No one would miss you
They'd all breathe a sigh of relief
to know that you're gone

I don't want to believe them
They're just a voice in my head

But they're loud
and persistent

How do I know
that it's not really me
saying these things?

After all,
aren't I the voice in my head?

How Are You Doing?

"Doing ok"
"I'm alright"
"Hanging in there!"

How do I tell you
that I'm hanging by a fraying thread
that I'm fighting for my life
that every moment
is both a struggle
and a miracle

Who really wants to know
that I'm lost inside my mind
being tossed by the currents
of shame and doubt
of grief and pain
of fear and worry

Losing hold of my lifelines
and struggling
to even want to try
to hold on tighter

Chapter 2

GRIEF

Grief isn't something you get to put off
until tomorrow
or next week

Grief lives in your bones

Grief

I'm no stranger to grief
We're quite well acquainted, actually

Grief isn't something you get to put off
until tomorrow
or next week

Grief lives in your bones
In the moments you have to remind yourself
they're dead now
you can't call them
and they certainly aren't calling you

Grief lives in the emptiness
you're forced to carry with you

When someone you love dies
the world seems to slow down
for a while

Time moves slower
and priorities shift
There's a tragic beauty to it
To the clarity it brings you

Yet somehow,
that clarity will leave you

and time picks back up
and you realize the world
never actually stopped

Only yours did

And you're left with nothing
but the emptiness

Survivor's Guilt

Birthdays are hard
when you're grieving
The phone calls you don't get
and the cards that don't show up in the mailbox
anymore

But more than the calls and cards,
you miss the people
Your family
Your friends
You still feel them
and their love
But it's not the same
Not anymore

There's a particular type of grief
in living longer than your siblings

I was 17 when Thomas died
He was 24

I was 26 when Austin died
He was also 24

Now I'm 28
and I carry a heavy guilt
A survivor's guilt

For being here when they aren't
For being 28 when they never will be
For the happiness I feel
despite them being gone

I know I shouldn't
I know they want to see me
happy
and alive

How I desperately wish
that I could see them
just the same

Angel Numbers

I don't believe in god
but I believe in people
and I think our souls
must go somewhere
when they leave our bodies

I'm at peace with not knowing for now
I'll find out someday

When my brother Austin died
I asked for a sign
so I could know
that he was still here
somewhere

He gave me that sign
I saw 999
3 different times
in less than a minute
Back-to-back-to-back
9 is his birth month

I felt with fierce conviction
that it had to be real
It had to be him
Even if it wasn't,
that's ok

It felt like it was
and that's enough
to help me get by

I see them everywhere I go now,
these angel numbers
and I can't help but smile

But I still felt the doubt
Until today, that is
I was walking back to work
and I saw a mother and daughter
sitting outside the Walmart parking lot
asking for money
I've seen them a few times
and it breaks my heart

I was carrying some leftover lunch
I debated silently
whether to offer them
my half-eaten lunch
I didn't have my wallet
and even if I did,
my wallet had no money
so it was all I had
to offer them

Would I want a stranger's half eaten lunch
in the midst of a pandemic?

Maybe not
but I'd appreciate the offer

As I neared them
weighing my options
a car drove by
the license plate ended with 333
and they had their blinker pointing
toward the mother and daughter

Without a second thought
I approached them
and offered them my lunch
and they accepted
and were grateful

Ironically,
the car didn't turn into the parking lot
I knew it was a message
from my angels
or theirs
so that they could receive what they needed
and so could I

The confirmation
that there is someone watching over us
but it's not god
It's ourselves
It's people

Looking out for each other
in this life
and the next

Chapter 3

AUSTIN

*I don't want you
living only in my memory*

Austin is my younger brother and one of the most important people in my life, which he has remained even in death. We lost Austin to an accidental overdose when he was 24. The shame and stigma surrounding drug use and addiction are part of the reason he's no longer with us. I wrote these poems as part of my ongoing grieving process, which I will be moving through for the rest of my life. I've chosen to share these poems as a way to honor Austin and help dismantle the stigma that contributes to preventable overdose deaths in any way I can, no matter how small. There is no part of me that is ashamed of any part of Austin. Even still, I've meditated on the question that perhaps this is not my story to tell.

But this is not Austin's story, this is a story at one of the intersections of his life with mine. This is *my* story of how losing him changed me forever — a loss that shook the foundation of my life at its very core. By telling this story, I extend the pieces of my broken heart out to the world with the hope that they reach the people who need to know they are not alone.

Austin

My dear brother, I miss you so
I don't know why you had to go
It isn't right, it isn't fair
This is a pain I never wanted to bear
Your whole life was ahead of you
I can't believe that this is true
I hold you close inside my heart
I wish that death hadn't torn us apart
I'm filled with rage and sorrow and pain
The grief is like a ball and chain
I miss your smile, I miss your laugh
With you gone I'm torn in half
I'm utterly lost, I miss you so
I don't know why you had to go
I know you're not the one to blame
You were a victim of their game
Brother, you deserved so much more
You were a victim of their war
My heart aches that you're not here
Some part of me still thinks you might appear
I wonder who you might have been, what you might have done
Your life had only just begun
You left a void that can't be filled
I know somehow I must rebuild
It feels wrong to leave you behind
Without you here everything is misaligned

I see you everywhere I gaze
Since you left, I've been in a daze
I'm filled with guilt from our times of strife
I'm furious that you lost your life
My dear brother, I miss you so
I don't know why you had to go

Fentanyl

It started out as a normal day
as it usually tends to
when your life changes forever

I was getting ready for an appointment
Dad called me twice while I was in the shower
The third call was coming through
as I stepped back into the room

"Hellooooo" I answered in a sing-songy voice
"Hellooooo" came back in response,
making me think that everything was normal

"What's up?"
"Your mom found Austin upstairs and he was cold"

My smile fades and my heart drops
"What?" is all I can bring myself to respond
*"She went upstairs to wake him up for work
and he was hard to the touch"*
"Like cardboard"
"Chyann... I think he's gone"

In that moment, my entire world
came to a standstill
Suddenly, I'm living one of my worst nightmares

"Austin OD-ed" I mouth to my partner
before returning to the call

"Did she call 911? Did the paramedics come?"
*"I'm not home yet, I haven't talked to her,
a neighbor called me"*
"Call me back when you know for sure"

The next call came in just a few minutes
but it felt like a lifetime

"He's gone, Chyann. He's gone"
I'm stunned into silence for a moment
"Was it fentanyl?" I ask
but I already know

*"That's what they think... I don't know, they won't let
me upstairs to see him"*
"GOD FUCKING DAMN IT"
I shout
not caring that it's my father's ears
that I'm screaming in

He can't be gone
He can't be

We have a quick exchange
about how soon I can be there
I have to reschedule my appointment

but I'm too hysterical to call
so my partner calls from the other room
as I scream and cry and beg and plead

How could this have happened?
Why did this have to happen?

It would be a few months from that day
until it was confirmed to be fentanyl
but I knew

I didn't get to see his body that day
They had to protect us from him,
but who was there to protect him
when it mattered most?

It doesn't feel fair
to know that he died alone
He died where it was supposed to be safest for him
and we'll never know
exactly when

I often wonder
if I could feel the moment
that he left
But it started out as a normal day

I'll never forget
watching them load his body into the van

The cruel irony of his body bag being green
His favorite color

I watched
in silent horror
as they took my brother's lifeless body
away from our home

I don't remember the day
he was brought home from the hospital
but I will never forget that day

Crying in the street
where we used to play
where we used to fight
clawing at each other's clothes
over who would get to sit in the front seat
of the family car

It all seems so small now
but I would give anything
to go back
to a time where I could take him for granted
because I didn't know
how little time
we really had

I Don't Want Them

When I drive my car
and look in the mirror
I see the Little Tree® that hangs there
that you bought for your own car

The car that's not in the driveway anymore
At the house that you're not at anymore

Every time I put on your sweater
I think of you
But then again,
I always think of you

I look at your trinkets on my bookshelf
Your pint of ice cream Dad made me take
because *"ice cream isn't ice cream without dairy"*
to him

At first, I didn't want to eat it
but I did
Still, I couldn't bring myself to throw the carton away
Because when I look at it, I think of you
But then again,
I always think of you

I think of the lessons that I've learned
since you left

The things I know now
that I might not have learned
if you were still here

But I don't want them

I don't want the lessons
the trinkets
the Little Tree®
the sweaters
I don't want you
living only in my memory

It doesn't feel right
to have your things
to know you're gone
I don't want them
I want you here

One Year

Here we are
on Father's Day
Dad's first without you
A year of painful firsts
after a year of unknown lasts

How strange it is
to come full circle
and feel so empty

We've each celebrated a birthday
Each another year older
Except you

Every holiday
a painful reminder
of your absence

How are we supposed to do this?
Year
after year
without you

It's been almost a year
since you've left
but it feels like
a lifetime

The day you died
is a day I've lived a thousand times

Each new day
puts me further away from you

The last time I saw you
The last time we hugged
The last time we spoke
The last time we fought
The last time you teased me
My last birthday with you
Our last Christmas with you

All drifting further
                        and further
                                            away

June 23rd

Tomorrow will be painful
because it's the anniversary
of your death

But I haven't been able to stop thinking
about how today is the anniversary
of your last full day alive

How different would things have been
if I had known

The last day I saw you wouldn't have been June 5th
The last day we spoke wouldn't have been June 14th

I would have told you
that I was upset
that you had bailed on our Father's Day plans
but that it's ok
and I forgive you
and that I'm glad we get to see each other
one last time

I would have hugged you tighter
I would have held you longer
I would have spent every moment
I possibly could with you

I would have been there that night
so that maybe you wouldn't die
and I wouldn't be writing this poem
I wouldn't be dreading tomorrow
I wouldn't feel so empty
so broken
without you

There was no way to know
I'd never see you again

There's no way to know
the last time we'll see anyone

So why don't we act like it
until it's too late

It Wasn't Supposed To Be This Way

It wasn't supposed to be this way
is something that I've said
countless times
since Austin died

In sober and somber moments
of grief and remembrance
In quiet, pained whispers
As well as loudly
and drunkenly
when I'm so consumed by the pain
that I can't contain it
and surrender to it

I've screamed it
Gasped it in shallow breaths
between sobs
Repeating it over and over
It wasn't supposed to be this way

I feel it
in the depths of my soul
That it wasn't supposed to be this way
That he should still be here

It didn't have to be this way
yet it is

So where does that leave me?
Stumbling through the rest of my life
without him

Trying and failing
to convince myself
that everything is unfolding
exactly as it should

Because if that's true
then he's supposed to be gone
and it wasn't supposed to be this way

A Secret

I have a secret
that I'm not proud of
but I have to honor these feelings,
visceral as they may be

I feel jealous
and sad
when I see someone
celebrating recovery

Please, don't get me wrong
I still feel happy for them
Truly, I do
The jealousy and sadness
are there because
I wish I could see Austin
reaching these milestones

1 year in recovery
3 years
5 years
10 years
50 years

Instead,
we're counting the years
since he died

I wish I could see him
healthy
and happy
and thriving
alive

Please, don't misinterpret
I don't wish that anyone
was in his place
I don't wish this pain
or loss
on anyone

I just have to admit
that it crosses my mind
any time I see a celebratory recovery post
Why can't that be Austin?
Didn't he
deserve this too?

Naloxone Can Reverse Opioid Overdose

Naloxone can reverse opioid overdose
Did you know that?
I certainly did
But I could do without
the constant reminders

In bar bathrooms
on billboards
and bus stops
and the buses
that drive by

Each one
a slap in the face
a painful reminder
that there are some overdoses
it can't reverse

Naloxone can reverse opioid overdose
so I carry it with me now
because you never know
when someone
might need it

But where was the naloxone
when Austin needed it?
And where was I?

Chapter 4

IN LOVING MEMORY

*They're still gone
and it doesn't end*

The Forget Me Nots

The forget me nots
are on my arm
for the ones I love
that I've lost
yet are just as much a part of me
as the ink now beneath my skin
so not to forget them
though I don't think I could
even if I tried
for they are woven
into every aspect
of who I am
From the features of my face
to the fondest memories in my heart
therefore always with me
even though we are apart
I don't need a tattoo
to remind me
to forget them not
but when I look at the blue blossoms
I can smile
and think of
my Nana and Poppy
my Grandma Toni
my Papa Wolf
my Uncle Rick
my Aunt Patty

my Aunt Kathy
my brother Thomas
my brother Austin
my cousin David
my friends Lizzie, Lupe, Conor, Tony, and Becca
and all those
I did not have the pleasure
of knowing in this lifetime
yet are the very reason
that I am here today

Thomas

My dear brother, I miss you so
I wish you never had to go
I wish I could have really known you
Our memories together are just too few
You had an entire life ahead
You've been gone so long instead
I hate to think of the pain you felt
I wish that wasn't the hand you were dealt
I wonder who you'd be today
I wish you never went away
I've held you close inside my heart
Since the time we've been apart
Time has helped to heal the pain
Yet I know some will always remain
To be older than you now doesn't feel fair
The guilt is sometimes too much to bear
I wish you could have met my son
Yet your life ended before his had begun
I wish I could remember your voice
You'd still be here if it was my choice
My dear brother, I miss you so
I wish you never had to go

Grandma Toni

I am eternally grateful for the time we shared
I feel deep gratitude for how much you cared
I wish you could see all that I've done
and where I am now
I wish I could see you, even once more, somehow
You were the crown jewel of our family
I hold you close in my heart tenderly
You taught me to love without condition
In my eyes, you are love's definition
If heaven is real, I know that's where you are
I just wish it wasn't so far
I miss you immensely and I will forever
Until the day we're back together

It Doesn't End

*Written in loving memory of the victims of the 2022
Club Q shooting in Colorado Springs
Daniel Aston, Kelly Loving, Ashely Paugh,
Derrick Rump, and Raymond Green Vance*

Some people say
that we're so desensitized to death now
but I'm not one of those people
who say that
and I'm certainly not someone
who feels desensitized

In fact, just the opposite
Sometimes I'd give anything to feel numb
instead of
whatever this is
because it doesn't end
and it somehow
only grows heavier

You don't have to know someone
to mourn them
and that's certainly true
with distant murders
that still hit too close to home

It's sinister to see the deaths
watered down to
compassionless stump speeches
viral posts circulating
cannon fodder for political debates
just another talking point

But these are real people
who are gone now

Someone's child
Someone's partner
Someone's parent
Someone's best friend

Someone
Someone
Someone
Someone
Someone

They're gone even when the news cycle moves on
They're gone even when the politicians
finish pandering
They're gone even when the viral Instagram posts
stop making their rounds

Even when the funerals are over
Even when you wake up the next day

and the next
and the next

They're still gone
and it doesn't end

Why It Matters

You get angry at me when I correct you
when you misgender or
deadname someone
You wonder why it matters
Why it's such a big deal

It matters because it tells us
you don't see us
you don't want to see us

It matters because it's not just that
It's also
the snide remarks
the judging glances
the stripping of our most fundamental rights
legislating away people's healthcare
depriving us of love
and acceptance
from our families
ostracizing us

It matters because
the only difference between all of that
and ending our lives in a hail of bullets
is how quickly it kills us

We Deserve To Live

I was at a gay bar a few nights ago
as I often am these days

As I watched people dance,
a thought came to me
The people who died that night at Pulse,
they were dancing just like this
It could be any one of us
at any time

I went home safe that night
and woke up to the nightmare
of another shooting,
this time in Colorado Springs

Five people didn't make it home
from a gay bar that night

Five beautiful lives lost
Countless lives altered forever

Then like salt
on an open wound,
the politics
the tired rhetoric
recycled thoughts
and empty prayers

Then even worse,
the silence
the indifference

It's not just these horrific events
of death and destruction
that haunt us

It's every moment
living in fear
that you
or someone you love
may be next

Every joke
that isn't really a joke
The laughter that hangs in the air,
ringing in our ears
long after the moment has passed

Every feigned concern,
which in reality
is just fear
and bigotry
projected onto us

It's my nephew
you still think is my niece
My ex-wife

you still call my ex-husband
It's the look my girlfriend gets from the pharmacist
when she picks up her HRT
the change in demeanor
the smile that was there just a moment ago
before the realization hit

It's the endless debates
Political debates
"Scientific" debates
Familial debates

It's the laws that hinder and harm us
growing ever stronger

It's the fear in my father's eyes
The disdain in my mother's voice
when she tells me not to correct her
She's trying
This is hard, ok?
This is new and confusing
to her
She should be *"allowed"* to deadname my cousin

The message of fear
and otherization
and hate
is loud and clear

We see it
We hear it
We feel it

That you would rather see us dead
or contorted to fit inside
the closets you built for us
than to see us live in a joyous freedom
you simply won't allow for yourselves
Continuing to bind us all
in these imaginary shackles

It's not just us that you harm in doing so
Can't you see that by killing us
you kill yourselves as well?

Who wants to spend their one precious life
terrified of the truest parts of who you are?

We all deserve to live our most authentic life
To be nourished and loved and fulfilled
To live without justification for doing so
on our own terms

We deserve to dance without fearing for our lives
We deserve to make it home
from a night at a gay bar

We deserve to live

long, full, happy lives

We deserve not just to live
but to thrive
freely
wholly
exactly as we are

Chapter 5

GROWTH, HEALING, AND SELF-LOVE

I am not something to be lost or found, I am simply here

Blur

Written August 31st, 2011

Who am I? Well I know not
I believe that's why I'm so distraught
A constant game of hide and seek
My cavity holds a heart so weak
So many emotions, yet none at all
A heart too big, yet far too small
Outgoing, loving, and fun?
Or angry, hopeless, and depressed?
I wish the latter could be repressed
I know who I want to be, but how
will I ever reach her?
The days with which I create myself
become nothing but a blur
Time is whizzing by me, slipping right
through my fingers
Yet I grasp on to the past.
My demons, they still linger
I don't know where I'm going, but I know I have to go
I'll have to be my own best friend, yet in turn
I'm my greatest foe
My fear was once that I had lost myself, but now
the truth is clear
I never truly knew who I was looking at
when I gazed into a mirror

Blur, Part II
Written December 12th, 2022

Who am I? I am constantly evolving
I am not a problem in need of solving
My soul is in a state of constant growth
My values are not set in stone, I've sworn no oath
So many emotions, that remind me I'm alive
With a heart full and strong, giving me
the strength to survive
Each part of who I am is worthy of love and adoration
Even — perhaps especially — the parts
that give me pause and hesitation
I know who I am, and I am already complete
Each new day brings me another version
of myself to meet
Life is a blur of joy and mundane, of love and pain,
of loss and gain
I am simply along for the ride, with no
control or domain
My fear was once that I had lost myself, but now
the truth is clear
I am not something to be lost or found,
I am simply here

A Love Letter To Myself

There's no one who knows you quite like you do
The love that you seek is always within you
You must be gentle with your own heart
The world is already trying to tear it apart
Forgive yourself for what you didn't know
Rejoice in the fact you continue to grow
Give yourself credit where credit is due
There's no one who knows just what
you've been through
Realize you're stronger than you like to admit
You've persevered despite wanting to quit
Nurture yourself because you deserve it
Affirm your self-worth and fiercely preserve it
It's fine to recognize where growth can be made
Don't sell yourself short though, that's now forbade
You have climbed mountains and put new life
on this earth
Even if you hadn't, you'd have the same worth
Don't let the patriarchal lies of capitalism
tell you different
Darling, you are simply magnificent
Never forget the power you hold
With time and wisdom it will grow tenfold
There is no need for external validation
Always view yourself with love and adoration
When you extend compassion, remember
to turn inward

For without compassion healing is hindered
You didn't deserve the pain that was inflicted on you
It's not your fault for what you went through
Remember that you're safe now and there can be peace inside
You can give yourself the protection you were once denied
Don't wish yourself away anymore
There's too much life left to explore
Too many versions of yourself left to meet
Remember you are already complete
You are the sun, the stars, and the moon
Beautifully emerging from your cocoon
Your life holds value which never expires
You deserve all that your heart desires
Look back gently at how you have grown
You will continue to reap what you've sown
You are worthy of love even if you forget
You are worthy of love even when you do things you regret
It's never too late and you're never too far gone
You can always return no matter how far you've withdrawn
Your brightness compares to that of a star
Marvel in gratitude at the wonder you are

27

One year older
One year wiser
Yet somehow,
I feel like I've lived many years
this particular year

I'll look back fondly
tenderly
on the growth and tears and joys
the triumphs
the love
the pain
all the small moments that I spent with myself
that were really the biggest moments of all

I'll remember this year
as the year that I came home to myself
and when I arrived there
there was a mirror instead of a front door
and I was shocked to find
that I never needed a key to enter

I'll remember this year
as the year I realized
that I have always been home

The year I decided to stay a while

kick off my shoes
put up some décor
and truly make my heart my home
safe and cozy

I owe everything
to the 26 versions that came before me
Who held me when I thought I was alone
Who stuck it out when I wanted to quit
Who made this year possible
The year I stepped into
my most authentic self

Where would I be
without their strength
resilience
and hope
that someday we might be here
on the other side of fear
on the other side of doubt

Thank you, thank you, thank you
Thank you for showing me
that I am the love of my own life

I'm Happy You're Here

I did an exercise
with my therapist
that involved
imagining myself as a child
and trying to feel
their feelings
of being a burden
of being in the way
of being a mistake
and oh boy, did I feel them

Then she told me
to hold my child self
and tell them
all the things
they needed to hear

So I sat with them
and I started to tell them
things like
"I love you"
"I'm here to take care of you"
I held them tighter
and began to think deeper
I told them
"You're not a burden"
"You don't have to earn my love"

"I'm happy you're here"

I had to stop for a moment
because I suddenly realized
what I've been needing to hear
my entire life

I'm happy you're here
I'm glad you're alive
You've done nothing wrong
You weren't a mistake

It was a powerful moment
and I haven't quite been the same since

Because now,
I'm happy I'm here

I'm In Love

I'm in love
with myself
and my life
and my friends

I'm in love
with the feeling
of sunshine
on my skin

I'm in love with
I'm in love with
I'm in love with the fact
that there's no limit to my love

I'm in love with the ocean
with the sound of the waves

I'm in love with my child
and their smile
and the feeling when they burrow
their head up against me
or ask to be held
I'm in love with the knowledge
that I am a safe place for them

I'm in love with the palm trees
and the sound the wind makes

when it dances through them

I'm in love with the view of the courtyard
through my office window
I'm in love with the dogs
that run and play there

I'm in love with my cat
In love with the way she loves kisses
and the way she curls up on my chest

I'm in love with softball
In love with the feeling deep in my bones
that says
'This is where you're meant to be'
when I step on the field

I'm in love with poetry
In love with the way
it connects me to myself
through time and space

I'm simply in love
with being alive
with this feeling
 — so new and refreshing —
of wanting to be here
(and meaning it)
of being deeply in love

with all the things
that make me human
that make me myself

Now the truth
gently dawns on me

I'm not simply in love
I *am* love

Beyond Survival

I was asked
by a therapist once
what my
overarching goal
of therapy
and life in general
was

I thought for a moment
before answering

"To survive depression"

It was my honest answer
at the time
and a goal I've
consistently met
so far

Lately though,
I've been pondering it
and I want to strive
for more
than just surviving

No

I want
to thrive

In spite of
depression
In spite of
it all

I want to thrive

28

Another year older
Another year wiser
Another year
that feels as though
several lifetimes
were lived within it

A particularly
turbulent
and challenging year
as I watched the stability
I'd built up over years
crumble beneath my feet

Yet here I am,
still standing

The year I learned
that stability
does not come
from the ground beneath my feet
from the roof over my head
from the job that I hold
or from the people
who may claim to love me
but rather
from a place

deep within me

I lost so much this year
and somehow still gained
more than I had once dreamed of
Surrounded by the safety
love
and support
of many beautiful friendships

I met myself deeper
and deeper still

Stopped running
from the beauty
and fullness
of who I am

Fully immersed myself
in my authenticity

What I once kept hidden
I now bask in

I've shed the weight
of shame and denial

I'll remember this year
as the year I finally realized

that it is my soul
that shines
at the center of my own universe

Bright and beautiful
Fierce and strong
A sight to behold
and a privilege to do so

The Best Is Yet To Come

On my college graduation cap
it says in sparkly gold lettering
The best is yet to come

Now that cap lives on my bookshelf
For a while,
I could only glare at it
Now,
it makes me smile

I'm In Love, Revisited

I'm in love
with myself
and my life
and my friends

I'm in love
with the feeling
of sunshine
on my skin

I'm no longer in love with ▪
and I love ▪
a little less each day
but I'm in love with the fact
that there's still no limit to my love
despite the heartbreak

I'm in love with the ocean
with the sound of the waves

I'm in love with my child
and their smile
and the feeling when they burrow
their head up against me
or ask to be held
I'm in love with the knowledge
that I am a safe place for them

I'm in love with the palm trees
and the sound the wind makes
when it dances through them

I no longer work in the office
with the desk that has the view of the courtyard
I no longer get to watch the dogs run and play there
But there are many places that I can go to do so
and I'm in love with that

I'm more in love with my cat
In love with the way she loves kisses
and the way she still curls up on my chest
despite how much she's grown

Now I have another cat
She, too, curls up on my chest
but she does not love kisses
and I'm in love with her

I'm in love with softball
(even more so now)
In love with the feeling deep in my bones
that says
'This is where you're meant to be'
when I step on the field

I'm in love with poetry

In love with the way
it connects me to myself
through time and space

I'm simply in love
with being alive
I hold on to this feeling
 — so precious and sacred —
of wanting to be here
(and meaning it)
of being deeply in love
with all the things
that make me human
that make me myself

Now I'm reminded
of the truth I had almost forgotten

I'm not simply in love
I *am* love
I will always be love
regardless of what changes around me

Chapter 6

THE JOURNEY HOME

*Now I live a life
I had never even dared
to let myself dream*

I Don't Agree

My mom called me recently
I was sitting at my desk
She wanted to let me know
that my family is worried
that sharing my queerness
is somehow putting my job in jeopardy
"You need to be careful with what you post online"
she says to me
"You need to be more worried about your career"
"Well, don't you agree?"
I can't say anything
because ironically, I'm sitting at my desk
But I don't agree
I don't think I should be worried about my career
I think I should be worried about
whether or not I'm happy
whether or not my family accepts me
or whether or not I'll make it home from a night out
with my friends
Because what good is a career that ends
on a blood-soaked dance floor
No, Mom. I'm not worried about my career
I'm scared for my fucking life

There Is No Closet

Inspired by Harvey Milk

I've been on a journey
of coming home to myself
for, well, my whole life really

I started to accept my queerness
when I was 21

I started calling myself queer
when I was 24

But I felt like an imposter
for a long time

I finally accepted that I'm a lesbian
at 28

I'll never forget
all those years ago
sitting in my college counselor's office
and telling him that I didn't want to
"make a big deal"
out of coming out as bi

"So don't" he replied
"I won't" I told him
and I didn't

But then something changed

I was on a precipice
in my journey

I was in a period of deep reflection
about gender
about queerness
about myself

I dove into queer media
and learned about Harvey Milk

I heard his words
*"If a bullet should enter my brain,
let that bullet destroy every closet door"*

They moved me
in such a way
that I started to feel
a sudden urgency
to come out
in this grand way

To let the world know
who I am
and live openly

Then my brother Austin died
and my priorities shifted
and I've also come to learn
that I wasn't quite ready yet

I still feel the burning desire
to live
openly and authentically
unapologetically

To be seen
and known
for who I really am

I still think about Harvey's words,
about how he was right
I think about how there were several bullets
that entered his body

I think about how we owe it to him
and to all those we've lost
to homophobic
and transphobic
violence
and to all those
who didn't get to live openly
when they were here
and to ourselves,
most of all

to live freely
wholly
as we are

I also think about
how it's more than just
letting those bullets
destroy the closet doors

I think about how
there is no closet
that we should allow ourselves
to be kept in
or feel the need to
come out of

Because there is no
default
or definitive way
to be human

We do not owe anyone
an explanation
or justification
of who we are
We can simply be

We are allowed
to change

to evolve
to grow
beyond what we once saw
as our limitations

To embrace oneself
is not to come out of a closet
but rather to stand firm
exactly where you are
exactly as you are

There is no closet

There is only you
and your boundless spirit

I'm A Lesbian

On December 24th, 2022
I finally said these words
out loud
for the first time
"I'm a lesbian"

Then I cried
in my girlfriend's arms
and when I finished crying
I sighed
and said again
"I'm a lesbian"

She smiled
and said
"Yeah, you are"
in such a way
that said
'It's about time you caught up on that one'

I began to think back on
all the years spent
on a long and lonely
winding road
that finally brought me here

To this moment

To this feeling
To this understanding

A lifetime's worth
of confusion and shame and denial
coming to an abrupt end
like shooting up in bed
from the fog of a dream
I didn't realize I was in

All those little moments
fleeting thoughts
lingering feelings
finally making sense

It felt like my world was spinning
for several days after that

Reliving my entire life
Seeing everything
in a whole new light

Reaching back through time and space
and finally piecing it all together

That I'm a lesbian
and always have been

The Fog

I recently came out to myself
Finally embraced
the parts of me
I had tried
desperately
to hide
and to bury
So much time
spent in a fog
All the while
being told
that the fog was the sunshine
and that I should be happy in it
Grateful for it, even
So engulfed and consumed by it
there was no way to know
that there was anything different
When you finally
step out of that fog
the true sunshine
brings a warmth
and sweet, gentle clarity
It shows you
all the things
that the fog had kept hidden
Shining its light
in all the places

where shadows of shame and confusion
once were
As you continue
to make your way
along life's path
beyond the fog
you slowly start to realize
that you were the sunshine
all along

Bloom

There's a term
'late bloomer'
but I don't subscribe to it
for a few reasons

One being that I am not late
I am right on time
my own time

Another being that I am not fully bloomed
and I don't think I ever will be

I will continue blooming
just as the universe
is constantly expanding

I'm Headed That Way Too

I didn't always know
that I'm a lesbian
In fact,
it was a truth
I fought against
for a painfully long time

But something in me knew,
somewhere deep within myself

I tried to tell myself
in a few different ways
One of those ways
was a dream I had

I was sitting in a park
a high school friend
began to approach me
carrying a lesbian flag
that billowed out behind her

She came to me
and told me that she was
carrying the flag
to celebrate
and acknowledge the fact
that her identity had moved

from bisexual
to lesbian

"I'm so happy for you!"
I told her
before pausing a moment
Then I said
"I'm headed that way too"

That dream shook me
to my very core

After that,
it was hard to keep running
from the truth
from myself

I was also right
I certainly was
headed that way too

Thank You, Faint Voice

When my relationship with my son's father
was reaching its end
I had begun to have the first stirrings
of thoughts that I might be queer

It was also in this relationship
that my first thoughts of nonmonogamy emerged,
though I hadn't put those pieces together quite yet

There were many reasons
that chapter needed
to come to a close,
the least of which being
my budding reckoning with my sexuality

But I can remember
a faint voice
from the deep recesses of my mind
that said to me gently
You will never fully figure out who you are with him

I didn't ignore this voice
but for many years I minimized
how important her wisdom was to me, even then
how crucial it had been
for me to hear those words

I think she knew
that she couldn't walk me across the bridge
that she could only lead me to it

It would take me many years from then
to make my own way
across the bridge
but I made it

Now I live a life
I had never even dared
to let myself dream

Chapter 7

TRANS: AN EVOLUTION IN SELF-ACCEPTANCE

*But my destiny was not preordained by the vessel that
contains my soul
and neither was yours*

Gender

My gender was given to me at birth
Bestowed upon me as if a gift
A calculated guess based on my anatomy
and with it, expectations of who I'm supposed to be
How I'm supposed to act
What I'm supposed to wear
Who I'm supposed to love
How I should do my hair
But my destiny was not preordained by the vessel
that contains my soul
and neither was yours
My gender is as expansive as the sea
and the only one who needs to understand it is me
I will never understand the gender of another
I was not meant to
Truthfully, I don't fully understand my own
My relationship with my gender fluctuates day by day
I may come to be a thousand genders before I die
and not a single one would be a lie
Gender is a feeling, an expression
It's a way to communicate something that cannot be
explained with words
Gender is malleable, fluid
Simply put, it's what you make of it
There are as many genders as there are people
I pity those that have trapped themselves in the boxes
that we try to fit our boundless spirits inside of

How small must their world be
How boring
Trapped in a prison of their own making
Shackled to a binary that only exists
in their minds

Trans

"When I look at you...
I don't see trans"
Someone I love
said this to me once
and I've said it to myself
quite a few times
But this is not
the right way
to look at being trans
So many transitions
cannot be seen
they can only be felt
and believe me,
I have felt them

Deadname

What's in a name?
I didn't think much of it
until my body
suggested to me
that I do
Until my name
began to feel
wrong

Would a rose
by any other name
smell as sweet?
More importantly,
would I be the same?
Would I be any different?

I can't quite put my finger on
what exactly feels wrong
Yet nothing else
— at least for now —
Feels like it would be
quite right

I don't like
'deadname'
as a term
as a concept

I never have
The morbid insinuation
and the cutting
of one version
of yourself
from another

It's not something
I want
to do
not something
I want to
understand
or relate to
But I can no longer deny
how it's begun to align
with my reality

Trans, Part II

"When I look at you...
I don't see trans"
Someone I love
said this to me once
but I don't say it to myself
quite as much
anymore

Not every transition
I've experienced
can be seen from the outside
but I've come to find
the evidence is more visible
if I know
where to look

It's more than just my hair
being shorter
or being colored
— though that's certainly part of it —
It's the difference in how I carry myself
in how much more comfortable I am
in my own skin
It's the way I've shed the weight
of shame
of societal expectations
of other people's projections

It's the self-love and confidence
that now pours out of me
when it was once kept dark and hidden

My experience of being trans
is not rooted in changing my external appearance
but rather in the internal acceptance
of who I've always been
and allowing myself to be
exactly that

Trans, Part III

For a lot of trans people,
being trans
is about making the outside
match what's inside

For me,
being trans
is about allowing myself
to feel what I do inside
regardless
of what's outside
and divorcing myself
from the expectations
that accompany that

Both experiences
are wonderful
and beautiful

Blissfully Chy

How silly to think
that this poem
is inspired in part by
my struggle in choosing
an Instagram handle

But that experience
only speaks to
a larger experience
in my transition

My name
has by far been
the most difficult part
of this journey
so far

In the beginning
it wasn't that
Chyann
necessarily
felt wrong
Chy
simply felt better
more fitting
a chosen name
blossoming

out of a childhood nickname

I chose
@supposedlychyann
because I had reached a point
where I didn't feel that
Chyann
fully captured who I was
anymore
I would joke with my friends
"Am I Chyann? Well, supposedly"

But then,
somewhere along the way
Chyann
did begin to feel wrong
and it slowly crept
toward becoming a deadname

So when I chose
@blissfullychy
it revealed
a very special piece
of my transformation

To move from something
I could only feel half-heartedly
to something I could feel
fully

Blissfully
Yes, Chy
That's who I am

Not Anymore

"What's your name?"

"Chy"

"Like the word?"

"Yeah, but spelled c-h-y"

"Oh, that's cool
Is it short for anything?"

I pause
I smile

"Not anymore"

I'm Not Dead Yet

As I've made my way
along the winding road
that is a transition
I've moved through
different feelings
in regard to my name

At times,
I've felt affirmed
by the term
deadname
and I do have to admit
that many of the feelings
I hold toward that name
align with this experience

But one simple fact remains
I'm not dead yet
and I have no interest
or desire
in "killing"
any previous version of myself

In fact,
I honor
and celebrate
each and every one

I respect the decision
of other trans people
to do so
but I've come to accept
that this is not my path

I have a birth name
a given name
a legal name
an old name
and I have
my chosen name

But no part of me
is dead

Not yet

House Of Cards

The framework of the colonial cisgender binary
aggressively attempts to have us believe
that the entirety of human existence
everyone who has ever existed
does exist
and will exist
billions and billions of people
fit neatly in two distinct, static genders
and that those genders
are predetermined by the body you're born in
But this framework is a house of cards
Because human existence
is much more expansive than that
The framework of my life
and the lives of countless others
the framework of our very being
is a complete and total rejection
of this feeble binary
Our mere existence
brings the house of cards
tumbling down

I Can't Keep This To Myself

When I first realized
and embraced
that I'm nonbinary
I shared it first
with my partner at the time
and told her that perhaps
I would keep it
to myself

Still suspended
somewhere between
cis and trans
in my mind

The discovery still too fresh
and so much still
to learn

People just won't get it
I remember thinking

That has been
the painful truth
for many years
and I imagine will be
for many more

But somewhere
along the way
I discovered that
this doesn't matter
as much to me
as standing
in my truth
regardless of how
messy or
confusing
it might be
to me
or anyone else

Somewhere along the way
I realized
that I can't keep this
to myself

Even later still
I realized
that I shouldn't have to

Chapter 8

THE SAPPHIC SERIES

I'll crave your skin against mine
Crave my hand on your knee,
our fingers gently intertwined

I Still Believe

My dearest love, my truest friend
I don't believe we've reached our end
I know that we're hurting from wounds old and new
But I still believe that my soulmate is you
I know that our pasts are afflicting us still
I know that this battle seems only uphill
But I don't believe there's a storm we can't weather
I still believe that we're better together
I know you have doubts, I have them too
But things that are doubted are often still true
I know that you struggle with thoughts hard to tame
I'm all too familiar with that gruesome game
I hope I can still be your light in the dark
You are still mine, I still feel the spark
We cannot know what the future might bring
But I do know that you make my heart sing
Darling, I know that it's frightening. Truly, I do
But I still believe that my soulmate is you

I'm Sorry

I'm sorry
that I wasn't ready
and for trying half-heartedly

I'm sorry
I want you to know
that it was all in my head
It wasn't you
or anything that you said

You didn't deserve
to be a pawn in our game
I regret it
every day

I miss our friendship
I miss you

I'm sorry
that I was ready too late
that she stood in the way

I wish
we really had a chance
to fail on our own terms

For My Love

My dearest love, I hope you know
The love we have will only grow
If life's a garden, you are the flowers
Blossoming after withstanding the showers
How lucky I am simply to know you
Luckier still to know a love so true
A love that can withstand the storm, the tides,
the tests of time
A love that is safe and sweet and sublime
A love that learns from mistakes that are made
A love that I treasure and would never trade
Evolving together, side by side
Two individuals beautifully intertwined
My love, you are a work of art
Thank you for trusting me with your heart
When I falter, I'll apologize
I won't hide behind my pride
If I hurt you, I'll repair it
I won't keep secrets, I'll be transparent
I'll keep you safe and love you fiercely
I make these promises from the heart sincerely
I won't make promises that I can't keep
I will sow love so love we can reap

Haunted By Your Ghost

It seems that I'm always waiting
on you
for one reason
or another
Waiting for a response
Waiting for a chance
Waiting on you to realize
how much you mean to me
Waiting for you to show me
how much I mean to you
Always waiting
Haunted by your ghost
Once, I was haunted by what we didn't have
What I couldn't say
Waiting
Yearning
simply to be with you
That time has passed
or has it only in my head?
Now I wait
to hold you again
to kiss you again
I don't have to wonder anymore
what your skin feels like against mine
Something I only used to dream of
Now I'm haunted by your ghost
Haunted by your razor in the shower

Your clothing in my drawer
Your toothbrush next to mine
Now I'm haunted by the things I did say
that didn't really matter to you
Haunted by the fact
that I fell in love with a ghost

My beautiful ■
I need you to know
there's nothing you need to prove
to anyone
Not even yourself
Give yourself
the love and adoration
you have always deserved
You don't need to wait
for anything
You are already whole
You are already beautiful
inside
and out
Even if you can't see it
Even if you don't feel it
It's still true
I promise you
You will only continue to bloom
into the beautiful flower
you have always been

████, Part II

I've been waiting
for the perfect moment
to say all the right words
in just the right way
with flowers in my hand
Truly, that was my plan
I've tried to tell you
in a million different ways
the words that I have yet to say
I've tried to show you
in the way I touch you
in the way I look at you
in the way I care for you
I've even tried to hide it
tried to bury it
Yet even then,
buried deep down
I still watered it
still nurtured it
Even buried, it never went away
Even buried, it only grew stronger
I can't deny it
and I don't want to
I don't want to wait
anymore
I don't want to hide
how I feel

about you
about us
I realize now
that every moment
has been the right moment
to tell you
that I love you

This is not a love that I fell into
It was more like
slowly waking up on a quiet morning
sunlight tenderly caressing my skin
gently wrapping me in a warm embrace
as we transition
from one state of being to another
A love that was found
in the exchange of hopeful glances
in the thrill of taking chances
in the stillness between passionate kisses
nothing but the sound of us breathing each other in
It seems silly to think
that there could ever be
uncertainty between you and me
Silly to think that I could ever doubt
To think I thought I could have gone without
Your love offered me shelter from the rain
A quiet understanding that I can't quite explain
The oceans in your eyes welcomed me
like a summer day
and darling, I think this gold might just stay

Love

I once thought that love was
the redness rushing to your cheeks
the heat beneath the skin
your heart pounding in your ears
that feeling in the pit of your stomach
as if you're falling through the sky

But I've found this not to be the case

Love is so much
softer
and sweeter
than that

Where there once was fire,
now there is calm
certainty

Love is safe,
grounded

Love doesn't make you question
or fear
or wonder

Love
ever so gently
makes its presence known

You're Safe With Me

New love is fun
and exciting
and then you reach a point
when new love
becomes real love
In those moments
where you show more of yourself
than you had before
and you're met with
a warmth
and tenderness
that tells you
'You're safe with me'
When the floodgates
built up over decades
come crashing down
your hand gently touches
my tear-stained cheek
and you don't have to say a word
yet still I know
that you're saying
'You're safe with me'
I let out a quiet sigh
as I rest my head in your hand
and you continue to hold me
as I'm swept away
by the waves

of grief and pain
and when they pass
you're still there
and the love in your eyes
tells me
'You're safe with me'
'Your heart is safe with me'
And darling,
I want you to know
Just as I am safe with you,
you're safe with me

One Night Walk

I saw her out of the corner of my eye
sitting alone at the bar
I sat down next to her
and I'll never be the same again

We got to know each other
walking the waterfront
in the middle of a perfect June night
Every moment together
genuine and pure
Our shared laughter
tenderly healing
We connected in ways
I had feared I may not be able to again

One night walk
with her
and I'll never be the same again

Crave

I had just a taste of you
but it was enough
to intoxicate me
Now I'll crave that taste
yearn for your whimper
dream of those brief moments
being tangled together
panting and gasping
tongues dancing
my fingers inside you
the words that you whispered
the words I whispered back
I'll crave your skin against mine
Crave my hand on your knee,
our fingers gently intertwined
I'll crave your head on my chest,
the tenderness of it
and how right it felt
I'll crave your smile
and the lips that make it
I'll crave you
until I can taste you again

But She's Out There

After ▮
I truly feared
that I would never
be able to
trust
love
or connect
with anyone
again

While those feelings
were painfully real
and understandable,
when I met ▮
I came to find
that they were not
grounded in reality

The ease with which
I connected with her
was a beautiful gift
and the brevity
of the time we shared
does not diminish
how impactful
or special
it was to me

I sometimes lament
about missing her
about wishing that there wasn't
so much distance
between us

On one such night
Nellie said to me
"She's so far away"

I let out
a melancholy sigh
before responding
"Yeah,
but she's out there
and that means other people
I can connect with
are out there too
and that's all I really need"

Chapter 9

HEARTBREAK AND RELATIONAL HEALING

*Or perhaps by that day,
I won't feel the need
to look back at all*

You Don't Deserve Another Poem

So I'm writing this one for myself
to commemorate this occasion
The day my heart caught up to what I already knew
so now I'm finally letting go of you
and the false hope I clung to by a fraying thread

Hope that maybe your lies were true
Hope that maybe the truth was a lie
But now the truth is simply too clear to deny

At long last, I can shed the layers
of hope and shame and love and pain

I can stop replaying it all in my head
wondering how it was that I was so misled

I can stop blaming myself
now that I'm unbound from your spell

I'm not a toy
you can leave on a shelf

My worth extends
far beyond
what I could be for you
The time to close the door
has been long past due

She was my first queer heartbreak
She was my best friend
but I wasn't hers
and I harbored
secret feelings for her
But it wasn't the 'falling for your straight best friend'
cliché
Though I almost wish it had been
That might have hurt less
No, instead I found out
she was *"experimenting with bisexuality"*
But before I could reveal
my true feelings,
she revealed hers
Feelings of disdain
Feelings of having grown
apart from me
Words that seared themselves
into my mind
and my heart
and have eaten away at me
through the years
Despite the pain,
I still think of her often
and wish her well
and wish it didn't have to end this way
or end at all

The Parking Lot

When I left your house that night
I walked past the exact spot we stood
in the parking lot of your apartment complex
where I told you I loved you
for the first time

As I stumbled through it this time
behind my tear-filled eyes,
I wondered if you really meant it
when you said it back that night

Then I sat in my car
a wailing, blubbering mess
giving myself the time I needed
before driving home

Like sobering up in the parking lot
after a night out
only much, much worse

The Aftermath

Just because you see something coming
it doesn't hurt any less
when it arrives
That's certainly true here
How surreal it was
to be curled up in your softest blanket
as you ripped my heart to shreds
My fruitless tears staining your pillow
as I tried and failed to make sense of it all
You didn't hug me goodbye when I left
For some reason, this stands out to me
because I know you hug your friends goodbye
and isn't that what we are now?
You told me to drive safe
but I didn't text you when I got back
Not to say I made it home
Not to say good night
Not to say I love you
I didn't text you good morning either
and you haven't texted me
It's strange
I'm not used to it yet
I wonder what you're feeling
as I fight back tears at my desk
Do you feel relief?
Do you feel as if
you've cleared your conscience?

Wiped your hands clean?
I hope that you don't,
but what does it matter?
What's done is done
We'll each feel how we'll feel
and live in the aftermath

Extinguished

I started writing you a poem
that I didn't get to finish

It was titled *A Slow Burn*
It was to detail for you
all the ways in which I loved you
and planned to love you
Because that was something
you had asked me to articulate for you
with no intention of doing the same for me

When I envisioned our relationship,
I pictured the slow burn of a candle
melting into a sweet, fragrant wax
Something to enjoy
for a long time to come
Not a spark that briefly ignites
and is quickly extinguished

Yet here I am
left behind in the darkness
of an extinguished love

Healing

I told you once
that it was healing
to be loved by you

You agreed it was the same
to be loved by me

Now,
I embark on the journey
of healing from you

"You're A Handful"

"She just didn't know
how to handle you
She wanted to get out of that
Come on, Chy
You're a handful"
My breath
catches in my throat
In that moment
my instinct
is to defend myself
To convince her
that it doesn't matter
how much of anything
she may think I am
that I didn't deserve the pain
of my heart being handled carelessly
She agreed
and apologized
and we laughed
carried on with the night
But the words
rattled around my brain
You're a handful
Hours later,
I'd wonder to myself
who among us
is not a "handful"

in their own way
and more than that,
what lover
wants empty hands?

When

Once
you hurt me
by how quickly you left

Now
you hurt me
by how slowly
you drag your feet
as you go

When
will you stop
hurting me

Trauma

"You see my trauma
and think that it's me
I see your trauma
and know that's what you aren't"

She's quiet for a moment
then says softly
"That's fair"

My heart sinks
Maybe it's fair for me to say
but nothing about it
is fair

"I Could Never Hate You"

You told me
countless times
that you could never
hate me

That was
until today
when you told me
you hate me
Doubled and tripled down on it

But the worst part was
that it wasn't news to me

It simply affirmed
what I had felt
for an excruciatingly long time

Ashes

Even if you burned
every bridge
between us
I'd use the ashes
to build another

Ashes, Part II

You burned
all the bridges
left between us
and it was foolish of me
to believe
that I could turn ashes
into stable ground

Even if I could
I'm not sure
I'd want to try
anymore

I'm afraid
I was wrong
about everything

There's nothing left
for us

Nothing left
of us

Nothing
but ashes

Chasing

She is always
chasing

Sometimes something more
Sometimes something less

And I am always
chasing her

Maybe
it's time
for us both
to rest

Simply Not True

Her words
had a greater impact
than I think she realized
They're etched
into my mind
deep in my heart
playing back
on an endless loop
"I'm so proud to be your life partner"
"You ungrateful piece of shit"
"Your lips are god's gift to this world"
"You're a horrible bitch"
"You're my soulmate"
"You fucking cunt"
"I love you"
"I hate you"
and the countless times
that I sobbed and begged
for her not to say
"Fuck you"
when we'd argue
I still can't believe
that she could say this to me
Often, as if it was instinctual
Forcefully, with malicious conviction
Easily, as if it brought her pleasure
"Too late, I already did"

would often be her response
It's hard to reconcile
or even understand
how all these words
came from the same person
A person who claimed
to love me more
than they'd loved anyone else
"You don't say these things
to people you love"
I told her once
"That's simply not true"
was her response
I suppose she was right
about one thing
Her love
was simply not true

I Could Never Hate You

I could never
hate you
Believe me,
I've tried

Even now,
after all
is said
and done
I can't find
any space in my heart
to hate you

It feels like
every day
there's a different future of ours
that could have been
that I find myself
mourning

It hurts to know
you don't feel the same
that you walked away
fed me hollow words
and empty promises
about love and friendship
about how this separation

doesn't need to be forever

How cruel of you
to put these lies in my mind
this false hope in my heart

Yet even still,
I could never
hate you

The Inside Joke

I was reminded of
an inside joke of ours
for the first time
that I can remember
since we split
It bubbled up
to the front of my brain
along with laughter
and joy
which almost
spilled out of me
along with the words
Until I remembered
there's no one here
to share them with
There's no more
shared laughter
no more shared joy
It stung to remember
that there's no more inside jokes
when there's no more us

Crawling Out Of Love

*"I've started
to put distance
between us
to protect myself
from getting hurt"*
she told me
at some point
months before the split

While I worked
to salvage
repair and
rebuild
what was left of us

I fought for that relationship
until its last breath
while she consciously chose
every day
to do the work
of detaching herself
from me
from us

Giving herself
the time
to move on

Pushing my opportunity
to do so
further
        and further
                back

Actively choosing
to fall out of love with me

I've been slowly
picking up the pieces
but I am certainly not
falling out of love

No

For me,
it's more like
crawling out of love

Painstakingly
crawling out of the hole
that she dug me in

The Sword & The Shield

We had a couple's therapist for a time
During our last session
they offered us some parting thoughts
They likened us to a sword and a shield
with me being the sword,
her being the shield
I didn't like the analogy then
and in the time since
I've reflected on the sentiment
quite a bit
Perhaps it never occurred to them
that a shield can easily be used as a weapon
but a sword
can hardly be used as a shield
Where did that leave me?

The Four Walls

"When I leave,
you'll have nothing
but the four walls"
she spat at me once
in a moment of anger

I don't even remember
what we were fighting about

It seemed as though
she was always
seeking to hurt me
with her words

She apologized
Perhaps quickly
Perhaps eventually
I don't remember how long it took

It doesn't really matter
Her apologies were meaningless
I don't know how she made
such empty words
feel so heavy

But how wrong she was,
that all I'd have

were the four walls

The walls and shelves
that we once shared
are now adorned
with pieces of me

There's a new set of shelves
to house my Pride hats,
ironically once kept
in the closet

My books and photos
trinkets and jewelry
the artwork I painted
with my own hands
are now on full display

It's taken some intentional time
but I've made this space
a new sanctuary
— a true sanctuary —
a place where I can feel
safe
and happy

I look around
and it brings me joy

It feels like a reflection
of me

Then I realize,
it is not the *things*
that truly matter

What matters
is that I finally feel at home
within these four walls

You Could Never Lose Me

"I don't want to lose you"
she said to me
many times,
tears in her eyes

I told her then
and it's still true as ever
"You could never lose me"

No, she certainly didn't lose me
For here I am,
still writing poems about her
with love for her
still in my heart

Still mourning us
Still missing her

She didn't lose me,
she discarded me

Intentionally
Maliciously
Callously
Pushed me away
and discarded me

It Has To Be Forever

*"It doesn't have to be
forever"*
she said to me once
"Really?"
I asked her
"You're open
to getting back together
someday?"
"Yes"

It was something
I held on to
A balm
for each wound
I was tending to
The old ones
and new

But her words and actions
rarely aligned
and I quickly realized
that it has to be forever

■, Epilogue

At first
there was a pain
that came
with the healing
her absence brought
There was a sorrow
within the peace
Doubts
that poked holes
in what I knew
to be true
deep within myself
I spent significant time
with my regret
with my doubts
with my pain and sorrow
It took some intentional time
but I eventually
became acquainted with them
asked them questions
of what it was
they were trying to teach me
Now they are old friends
who sometimes come to visit
but I no longer dread
their arrival
I let them move through me

and let them teach me
how to forgive myself
and let go
of all I thought
it could be
and embrace what it is
My new beginning
and all my new chances
to become more acquainted
with my healing
and peace

Imagine

I look at photos of us
I look at myself
My smile
so sincere
The look of contentment
on my face

Sadness gently embraces me
I do not push her away

Instead,
we reframe the feeling

If I could be
that happy
that content
when things were hard
when love hurt
with the wrong person

Imagine
how happy
and content
I will be
when things are light
when love heals
with the right people

Sadness holds me close
and whispers
Imagine

Then she walks away,
leaving hope
in her wake

Walk Away

I'm the type of person
who stops to talk
to mall vendors
*"You stay longer
than you need to
You need to learn
to just walk away"*
she'd tell me in annoyance
I've been thinking a lot
about this lately
I don't have any regrets
of staying to talk
to a mall vendor
for too long
but I have countless regrets
of staying with her
for far longer
than I should have
It turns out it was her
I needed to learn
to walk away from

If Looks Could Kill

We saw each other briefly
My smile was weak
but I still gave it to you

Your glare was crystal clear
even beneath your sunglasses

In one moment
a year's worth of hope
that someday we could be
even just cordial strangers
disappeared

If looks could kill
I would have died in that moment

But then again,
if looks could kill
I would have died a long time ago

Pull The Plug (Again and Again)

I don't remember
what her question was
but my answer was
"Because I love you"
"Well stop!"
she yelled at me
"Pull the plug!"

I didn't know then
and I still don't know
how one can simply
"pull the plug"
on a love
as deep as the love
I felt for her
or how long it might take
to drain an ocean

I read somewhere recently
that when you love something deeply
you will need to let it go
many different times
again and again
I have found this to be true

I have pulled the plug
I have let her go

many times
again and again
but it all comes
and goes
in waves

Sometimes I can sail
the ocean smoothly
while other times
it feels as though
I'm drowning

But ever so slowly
the ocean grows smaller
each time
I pull the plug

Though right now it feels
far away
I know there will come a day
when I will pull the plug
when I will let her go
for a final time

The ocean will fully drain
and perhaps on that day
I might be able to look back fondly
Or perhaps by that day,
I won't feel the need
to look back at all

Chapter 10

COMMUNITY AND FRIENDSHIP

*Words fail me
in trying to explain
exactly how special it all is
But I want them to know*

Where Are You?

*"There are so many people
who are going to love you
that you haven't met yet"*
So the saying goes
I try to remind myself
when things are hard
and the feelings of loneliness
grow heavy
Where are you?
my heart calls out to them
I'm ready to love you too

Kathryn

Kathryn
is a special friend
One of those friends
that can always
lift your spirits
warm your heart
make you smile
With a knack
for often saying
just what you need
to hear
Always
so gently
and lovingly
I once viewed Kathryn
as the silver lining
from a painful relationship
Well,
I'd tell myself
at least I met Kathryn
Though I'm grateful
beyond words
to have met her
I quickly
unlearned this silly thought
Kathryn
and her friendship

are much more
than a silver lining
More precious to me
than gold

"I Hope You Have Someone Good"

It's a Saturday night in my Lyft
I pick up some drunk guys downtown
Not too drunk
and they turned out to be very nice

We chat
Tell embarrassing drunk stories
My story involves an ex-girlfriend
and something she said
while she was breaking up with me

At the end of the ride
we're saying goodbye
One of the guys says to me
"I hope you have someone good"
and off they go
down the alley

I look after them
smile to myself
partially just relieved
a ride with two drunk guys went so well
It's also sweet and touching to me
that he would say this
I hope you have someone good

But then my heart begins to sink

thinking I don't really "have" anyone
at least not in the sense that I think he means

But then I think of Kathryn
I think of Debra
of Jess and Nellie
Christina
Althea
and Shelby
I think of Becca
of Burkie
I think of Quinn
of Ryan and the cats
of my parents
suddenly turning a corner
in accepting my queerness
I think of my brother Aaron
of Ann and Leanna
Linda
Monique
Jamie
Laura
Erin
and Victoria

I think of the beautiful community
that surrounds me
uplifts me
loves me

accepts me
celebrates me

Then I think of myself
and I realize,
I have so much more than just good

I drive away
heart soaring
thinking of how lucky I am

What I Want My Friends To Know

I want them to know
how deeply
and sincerely
I love them

I want them to know
how special they are
Not just to me,
but to this world as well

I want them to know
how much their love
fulfills me

How warm it makes me
How safe it is
How precious

I want them to know
how much I appreciate
and adore them
How beautiful they are
How bright they shine

I want them to know
how much I cherish
the tender intimacies

we share

When they put their arms around me
to keep me warm

When we embrace
to say hello and goodbye

The way we squeeze each other
The way we sometimes
start to stop
then continue embracing
just a little bit longer

The "love you!" we exchange
when we part ways

Playing with each other's fingers
Gentle shoulder massages
Endless laughter

The tears in my eyes
when I bare my heart to them
The love that reflects back to me
in theirs

Words fail me
in trying to explain
exactly how special it all is
But I want them to know

Community

It's been on my darkest days
that community
has shined the brightest
as if to remind me
that love and beauty
will always remain

Alien

For Noelle

If you're an alien,
well then I'm an alien too
Maybe not the same kind
of alien as you
But as far back as I can remember
I've struggled to fit in
Fit into my family
Fit in with friends
and the friends I made
looking back, a lot of it feels pretend
I never knew how to describe it
when I was growing up
I just felt
different
Like you said...
alien
I didn't think the same
I didn't feel the same
I couldn't be the same
Now I see it for the gift it is
the strength it is
the beauty it is
But there is a pain
looking back
at all the times
I tried to make myself fit

where I didn't belong
But if you're an alien
and I'm an alien
I guess I was just waiting
for more aliens to come along

Chapter 11

LOVE AS A LENS

*How could I possibly
explain
what your heart
already knows?*

Untitled

Each new day could be our last
Becoming a permanent part of the past
In this life, the only guarantee is its end
Death is not something we've found
a way to transcend
Even in all our hubris, advancements, and delusions
Why then do so many spend their life stuck
in false illusions
We have such short and precious time together
During this storm called life we must weather
Why inflict more pain on each other when we
could all thrive
Yet so many scrape by just to survive
I dream of a world that is peaceful and flourishing
Where everyone's priority can be
their soul's nourishing
A world without hunger, poverty, or war
A world in which we empower each other to soar
A world without capitalism, austerity, or greed
A world in which we all have what we need
A world in which nobody sleeps on the street
A world with no classes; no poor or elite
Because you see, we all have the same worth
Which we've all held since the time of our birth
Nobody has to earn love or a home or their food
How did this life get so misconstrued

I dream of a world without prisons, patriarchy,
or racism
A world in which no one feels the need for escapism
A world filled with love, compassion, and care
A world that is equitable, just, and fair
A world with no sexism, ableism, or violence
A world in which nobody suffers in silence
A world without discrimination, imperialism,
or the hoarding of wealth
Where everyone has the same access to care
for their health
I dream of a world in which we abolish the binaries
of sex and gender
Where everyone can live their most authentic life
in splendor
For now these are dreams but someday they'll be real
I hold on to the hope that someday we will heal
Right now we can't grasp the magnitude
Of how we'll marvel in wonder and gratitude
At the world that we built with devoted commitment
We must sow love now so we can reap the fulfillment

I Get Angry

I get angry
when I see the tents
lining the sidewalks
When I see people
sleeping on the streets
or sitting on corners
and at intersections
holding up cardboard signs
for even a chance
at some spare change
maybe a few dollars
or some food

I get angry
Furious, even
But not at them

No

I get angry
at the people with the power
to end this
who continue to allow it
as well as those
who continue to profit from it

Day after day

Night after night

Human beings
sleeping outside
dying outside
as houses sit empty

Yeah, I get fucking angry
at the empty promises
at the lies
the pandering
the greed
at the complete and utter
lack of humanity

How fucking dare they
point their fingers
dripping with blood
at the victims
of their willful complicity
and blame them
for their own suffering

Stealing
or destroying
what little they own
Stripping away
every chance
they might have had

Pushing them
deeper into despair

How evil
do you have to be
to put a tent
that someone calls a home
into a trash compactor
before their very eyes

These are real people
simply trying to survive
fighting an uphill battle
with manufactured obstacles
placed in their way
by those who claim to be helping them

Displacing someone
to the adjacent sidewalk
helps no one

Every day
people die
on the streets
and sidewalks
of this city
Some nameless victims
because they lost their identification
in the most recent sweep

While the Mayor's administration
has the audacity
to brag
about how much they've accomplished
and harasses anyone
who dares to disagree

Drive through the streets of downtown
and see for yourself
just how much
this administration has done

Miracles

When I think of this world
This beautiful, random world
Born out of space itself
This spinning rock
orbiting a dying star
flying through space
faster than our minds
can even comprehend
With air we can breathe
Food that grows
from the earth beneath our feet
With beautiful mountains
and oceans and trees
Perfect and wonderful
An absolute miracle
I wonder why
Why
can't we just enjoy it
Enjoy this miracle
of a planet
and each other
Each miracles
in our own right

How Can I Explain?

My worldview
and ideology
make perfect sense
to anyone
who believes
in the interconnectedness
of all beings

How could I possibly
explain
what your heart
already knows?

When It Rains

I've never liked the rain
Some people find it "cozy"
but this has never
made any sense to me

You do not stand in the rain
and call it cozy
You call it cozy from inside
A privilege
so many people
do not have

When it rains
I think of Gaza
I think of the displaced people
Some living in tents
Some living without even a tent

When it rains
I think of San Diego
I think of my homeless neighbors
Also living in tents
Also living without even a tent

When it rains
I think of all the people
without a roof

or warm clothes

When I change out of my
rain-soaked clothes
and put on warm, dry clothes
I think of Palestine and Sudan
and homeless San Diegans

I get into my bed
and I think of them
I feel guilty
for having my warm clothes
for having my bed
for having my roof
when too many people
have none of these things

I try to reframe the guilt,
but it is hard to do
It's not that I don't deserve it,
it's that they do too

I think of all the empty houses
Homes that people fled
Homes that are destroyed
Homes that people
couldn't afford anymore
and were evicted from
Empty vacation rentals

that someone could call home
but someone else's greed
prevents them from doing so

No one
in any part of the world
should be forced
to sleep or live outside
even when it's not raining
But it is raining
and I think of them

"Be Grateful It's Not You"

"Be grateful it's not you"
"Remember,
it could always
be worse"

These are philosophies
that my soul rejected
from the time
I was a young child

Viewing gratitude
through the lens
of other people's suffering
has never
and will never
sit right with my spirit

Even before I had the words
to articulate it,
it's something that was written
into the fibers of my being

I will never find
joy, peace, relief, or gratitude
when I look at the suffering
of another

Rather than being grateful
it's not me,
I interrogate
why it has to be them

At The Altar Of A New World

A better world is possible
A mantra
that I've repeated
many times
throughout my life
and I am not the only one
A truth
I believe
in the depths of my soul

A better world is always possible
But a safer
more just
and harmonious world
will not come to be
without sacrifice

Thomas Sankara once said
"We must choose either
champagne for a few
or
safe drinking water for all"
I've made my choice
and I am willing
to lay down
every privilege I hold
at the altar of a new world

I have come to find
that comfort cannot truly comfort me
knowing it comes
at someone else's expense
Their comfort
Their joy
Their health
Many times, even their life
I am not willing
to accept this

Innocent people
have unjustly lost their lives
at the altar of capitalism
at the altar of imperialism
at the altar of hate and greed
at the altar of death and destruction

It never needed to be this way
and I hold on to the hope
that it won't always be
A better world is always possible

Chapter 12

WRAPPING UP (UNCATEGORIZED)

*I've been trying to say
the things I need to say
more often
even when it's difficult
and scary
and I hope you do too*

Dad

I hope you always know how much you mean to me
The memories that you helped us make
live in my heart so tenderly
You've always been there, with unconditional
love and support
Attending every concert and play, cheering us on
for every sport
Every relationship experiences peaks and valleys and
ours is no exception
Yet even so, it's nice to know that now we're at
a peak in our connection
I hope you always know that I don't take
a single moment for granted
Even the moments that aren't quite so candid
Because each and every moment has made each of us
who we are
Without you and you've all done for me, I don't think
I would have made it this far
I hope you know how much you are appreciated,
for who you are not just for what you do
A father is a special person and I'm so glad that mine
is you
Thank you for instilling in my brothers and me
a deep, undying love of family
To see you as a grandparent is a privilege and an honor
I hope you always know how proud I am
to be your daughter

Ryan

My sweetest love, I love you so
More than you will ever know
I've never shared a bond like this
Thanks to you I know true bliss
Even when times get hard and we may fight
I will always love you with all my might
I promise to keep you safe and protected
I promise you'll be heard and respected
I promise to nurture you through the years
I'll be there to witness your tears
You can trust me with any emotion
I'll care for you with loving devotion
My dear, you a wondrous being
Receiving your pure love has been beautifully freeing
You've taught me more than I could ever expect
About life and love and joy and respect
You deserve the world and more
I cannot wait to watch you soar
You are my very best friend
My love for you will never end

Serena's Lesson

My dad has a boat
Her name is Serena
and she taught me an important lesson
on letting go

Or rather,
I taught myself

We were trying to honor my brother
with a paddle out
but things didn't go according to plan

Some of us took Serena out past the break
and were going to paddle in
toward those who were paddling out
from the shore
Three of us were supposed to jump
into the water
and onto our paddle boards
But I was afraid
to jump in
so I tried to step down onto the board

Serena was moving with the waves
Rocking us back and forth
Up and down
I tried to step on the board

but it started to drift away

I held on to Serena with all my might
as my legs pulled away with the board
"Jump!"
"Let go!"
the calls came from the deck

I was scared
but in the end,
I did jump

The paddle out didn't go as planned
Those of us who were out there
were tossed by the waves
and immediately went back to shore
My dad stayed on Serena
so he wasn't even there

We didn't get a chance
to honor Austin
in the way we had hoped
and I was left with
a bruise on each arm
from holding on to Serena
when I needed to jump

And this was her lesson:
That it hurts more to hold on
than it does simply to let go

Eggshells

I'm tired
of walking on eggshells

I'm ready
for the freedom
to run
to dance
to fall
to live

I Hope You Tell Them

I've been trying to say
the things I need to say
more often
even when it's difficult
and scary
and I hope you do too

When you love someone
and you're not sure
if it's "too soon"
to tell them
I hope you tell them

When you think a stranger
has a nice smile
or beautiful hair
I hope you tell them
and make their day

When someone hurts you
I hope you tell them
and I hope they tell you
that they're sorry
and mean it
and if they don't
I hope you know
you'll still be ok

I hope you tell people
that they're beautiful
or fun to be around
I hope you tell them
that you miss them
or admire them
or love them

I hope you tell them when they help you
with figuring yourself out
or overcoming a fear
or getting over something
you never thought you could
I hope you tell them how much that meant to you
Because I promise you
they need to hear it

If you have an old friend
that may have hurt you
that you haven't spoken to
in a long while
that you're missing
I hope you tell them
and I hope they miss you too
Because I hope she misses me
and I hope I tell her someday

It's not always easy

to say what you need
or say that you're hurt
or say that you're sorry
But I hope you tell them
while they're still here to tell

Small Things

The more
small things
I do
the more I find
that the small things
are actually
the big things

Radical Dreamers

"I'm a radical dreamer"
I say to Jess

She chuckles softly
*"I'm glad you've acknowledged
that these are just
dreams"*
she says back to me

I want to keep this moment alive
I want to let it fuel me
I want to come back to it
again and again

Because someday
when all of my dreams
are reality
I'll look back
and I'll chuckle softly to myself

Oh, Jess
Don't you know
that we're all radical dreamers?

The difference between us
is what we're willing to do
to make those dreams come true

I'm Not Afraid

I'm not afraid
to admit that I'm
a sensitive soul
I've come to find
the strength
and beauty in it
and will no longer
apologize

I'm not afraid
to let it be known
that I am deeply moved by life
by its beauty
by its tragedy
by all its wonder
and mystery
I'm not afraid
to let it transform me

I'm not afraid
to admit when I'm hurt
to admit that I've caused hurt
to admit when I'm wrong
to admit that I care
What I fear more
would be to not care

I'm not afraid to cry
I'm not afraid to *feel*
I'm not afraid of my emotions
I've opened myself up
to let them teach me
Because I'm not afraid to grow
even when it's painful

I'm not afraid
to admit that I'm often
terrified
anxious
unsure

There are many things I do
with a racing heart
and sweaty palms
but I do them anyway
because I'm not afraid
to do them afraid

Acknowledgements

- To the generous and supportive members of my community who donated to help make this book possible, I extend my deepest gratitude to each of you: Olivia, Noelle, Cristal, Christina, Caty, Laura, Althea, Ann, Amanda, and Erika.

- To my chosen family, who know who they are. Thank you for loving me as I am and continually lifting me up and pushing me forward. I love each of you and the unique joy you bring to my life. This book would not exist without the love and support you give me every day. From the bottom of my heart, thank you for being you and thank you for finding me.

- To Kathryn, thank you for your unwavering support in everything I do. Your love helped me to move through so much doubt and imposter syndrome. Thank you for your patience as I asked for your opinion countless times, all the times you helped me work through a decision, and for your thoughtful and sincere advice. You were a large part in making this book what it is. I thank my lucky stars for you and our friendship every day.

- To Noelle, thank you for being the first person to ever read this book. Thank you for your support and encouragement as I began the publishing process, for the patience and love you extended me in times of uncertainty, and for being a reliable sounding board when I needed it.

- To Tris, thank you for bringing my vision for the cover art to life so beautifully and dynamically. Your talent and unique touch made it something truly special. I feel honored to share this publication with you and have our respective art out in the world together.

- To Sunny and Anthony of Poets Underground Press LLC, thank you for seeing and supporting my vision. Thank you for guiding me through the process of publishing my first book and helping me become a stronger and more thoughtful writer along the way. Thank you for creating the Poets Underground community, where we poets can share tender vulnerability, connect, and grow together. I am forever grateful.

Meet the Author

Chy Cox (they/she) was born and raised in Oceanside, California and now happily lives in the University Heights neighborhood of San Diego, California. They started writing poetry in 2010 as a sophomore in high school and began performing at open mics hosted by Poets Underground in 2022. Since then, they have performed their poetry as a featured artist at Art of Pride's "Art Show!" in 2024, at the 2024 San Diego Pride festival, and in the inaugural installment of the local Calm & Queer monthly series created by Janine Rose in September of 2024. Chy's first publication appears in the second Poets Underground anthology Still Here. Through Time and Space is her debut full-length collection. Along with poetry, Chy's passions include performing as their drag king persona, Chy Guy, with the San Diego Kings Club, playing softball, and making memories with their loved ones.

Meet the Publisher

Poets Underground is a Movement
Sunny & Anthony Azzarito, the Founder/CEO and COO of Poets Underground Press LLC. Their passions drive from their love for God, their 5 children, their inclusive community and the arts. The couple runs writing events, open mics, writing & preforming workshops, retreats, partners with schools and community service events; in great effort to foster healthy individuals and communities. Known for their partnership publishing programs, they welcome all aspiring writers to apply.

poetsundergroundpress.com

Index

"These words are all I have, so I write them"
Fall Out Boy
Dance, Dance (2005)

"If a bullet should enter my brain, let that bullet destroy every closet door"
Harvey Milk
November 18th, 1978
Recorded on a tape that was to be played in the event of his assassination

"We must choose either champagne for a few or safe drinking water for all"
Thomas Sankara
1986

POETS UNDERGROUND

Made in the USA
Middletown, DE
01 December 2024